Dec. 9, 2018

Dear —

Here it is, my friend!

I hope you enjoy these words.

Much love brother.

Jackson

Becoming

Jackson Maloney

Jackson Maloney

Original title
Becoming

Front cover image & design, inside images
Jackson Maloney

Front cover editing
Mitch Wenig

Back cover image
Thomas Maloney

Layout
Yossi Faybish
Sonja Smolec

Published by
Aquillrelle

© Copyright Jackson Maloney, 2018

All rights reserved. No part of this book may be reproduced, stored in a retrieval system or transmitted in any form or by any means without the prior written permission of the author and publisher. Quotes of brief passages may be reproduced in a newspaper, magazine or journal for reviews only.

Printed in the United States of America.

ISBN 978-0-359-09559-9

"The mystery cannot be controlled. That can be scary. When I can surrender to the mystery, the unknowing, I am in harmony, no longer in opposition, to that which includes the mystery of myself."

Dan Surface

"What has no shadow has no strength to live."

Czeslaw Milosz

This book is dedicated to Taylor Nicole King, whose fierce love cut me open.

Table of Contents

Part 1 Becoming Honest

A New Beginning..13
Trust..15
On My Last Breath..17
This Is It...21
Mother Earth..25
Sunrise Over the Sangre de Cristos......................................27
The Voice of Poetry..29
Becoming Honest..31
The Last Night We Made Love 33
There is a Hole in My Heart...35

Part 2 Becoming Alone

Washing a Spoon..39
Dried Up..41
What You Are Becoming 45
From the Fire..49
Sitting Outside Before Dusk...51
The Work...53

Our Fathers 57
Old Knowledge 63
Dragonfly 65
Surrender 67
Moving Towards Life 69

Part 3 Becoming Home

My First Garden 73
Welcoming You In 75
Beneath the Fire 77
What We Deserve 79
Sea Glass 83
What Is Carried 87
Passing a Crowd of People by Car 91
Arête 93
My Body Is My Prayer 97
Crows 99

About the Author 109

Part 1
Becoming Honest

Becoming

Jackson Maloney

A New Beginning

Down beneath the house
in the cold, ripeness of morning,

there is a secret dwelling
place – old and timeless,
stretching through the darkness
as stars that guide the people.

What is it in you
that needs a new beginning?

What quiet, fragile song
is whispering
in the wee hours before dawn

asking courageously to be carried
from the protective cradle of night

into the bright, open
waiting day?

Becoming

Jackson Maloney

Trust

I have deep, unexpressed urges
weighted like a breath held in.

They swirl around in some
hidden chamber of my heart,

gated off like a pirate's cove,
lurking in the still, black waters.

This is the cave of my unconscious,
I have been waiting
to stumble into,

and finally,

I find myself lost
far enough inside the darkness
paddling like a drowning dog,
that the only option I have
to live

is to let my last breath go,
and duck my head down under.

Becoming

Jackson Maloney

On My Last Breath

There is something heavy
like a wave
wanting to fall
through me,
but I clench my body
so the water cannot reach
the roots.

I am dying
like a tree that has dropped
its fruit,
but I am still so young,
and there is more give.

What is life?
I want to know.

The footsteps back
from where I came
are disappearing
in the shadows of
the night.

I sit alone now
with the shadows
slipping like a veil
over the mountain
afraid to let go
into the black face
of my unaddressed grief.

That is where the water
I am seeking lies stagnant.

Becoming

Jackson Maloney

That is where something
is waiting
to be born.

That is where
I must go.

Becoming

Jackson Maloney

This Is It

You can push
and push and push
to get everything you think
you want
to get to that place
you think you need
to go
meanwhile
you slowly blind yourself
to everything
you already have
around you
to all the people
who already love you
as you are
until at some point
there is
a significant loss
which cuts you open
like a shovel blade
in the soft earth
so exposed in the face
of other creatures
so raw
so real
because for the first time
you see your life
as it really is:
a fragile bead
of water
glinting

Becoming

Jackson Maloney

in the sun
sliding down
a single blade
of grass, back
into the dirt.

Becoming

Jackson Maloney

Mother Earth

When I was breaking down,
you gave me yourself
hollowed out,
so what was heavy in me
had a place to return.

Becoming

Jackson Maloney

Sunrise Over the Sangre de Cristos

The calm, blue bosom
of early dawn
turns to fire
at sunrise.

I watch the sun's
slow entrance
with the sudden,
insurmountable fear
of how one day
I will watch
my last sunrise
and go somewhere else.

How little I know
about death!

Those black branches
of hands,
waiting,
the open mouth
taking my shape.

I want to live!

Becoming

Jackson Maloney

The Voice of Poetry

It wraps itself
in shapeless wind,

flooding through me when I walk
into wide and open spaces,

unfurling itself like a wild tiger.

It curls low along the ground
so that I must bend down to hear it,
barely audible,

like a song at the bottom
of the throat,

trying to find an opening
out of the darkness.

It hides beneath the cover
of tall pine

along a quiet back road,
waiting to be discovered

like a child playing
hide and seek

who finally surrenders
to the urge to be found

and walks out freely, excitedly,
from the safety of the shadows.

Becoming

Becoming Honest

It takes courage to ask the questions
that might shatter your heart
into a thousand fragile pieces,
but you do it anyway, because
it is the true way, the only way
to move through the hurt
you have harbored too long.

Now, you are ready to face
what is real
beyond the story of your pain,
so you put down
your weapons
of defense,

and humbly ask
the questions
that have haunted you like a ghost
and open
as best you can
to the answers
you never wanted to know.

Becoming

Jackson Maloney

The Last Night We Made Love

I have never felt the power of impermanence
the way I did the last night we made love,
and I wept rivers amongst the other fluids
moving, so that our bodies were swimming
in all the juices we could muster,
and when we reached the ocean of one
another we became waves
rising to meet each other at the peak
before collapsing back under together
and that was all I needed
to see that these forms do not last forever
and as overwhelming as my sadness came after
with the truth of our separation
it was the most honest moment of not knowing
where I ended and you began
where union between life and death
was being created by you and me
and it was ok to finally let go.

Becoming

Jackson Maloney

There is a Hole in My Heart

There is a hole in my heart
where you used to live.

It took
two years
to see I was using you
to avoid falling in.

Now that you are gone,
that hole has grown arms
of its own,

and they are pulling me

down.

Becoming

Part 2
Becoming Alone

Becoming

Jackson Maloney

Washing a Spoon

I lean against the dark wood
of the kitchen counter
to wash a spoon.

The sun rising
through the east window behind me
has warmed up the wood,
and I feel the warmth against my pelvis
as I push up against it to reach the water.

I want to stay there,
in that feeling of comfort I knew with you, too.

I have never felt this alone;
so vulnerable to morning,
so open to my life.

I am looking for a word
to describe it to you:
clouds bulging in a storm,
wet dirt, clear light bouncing
off running water. A hand

lain open in the dark
ushering me in.

Becoming

Jackson Maloney

Dried Up

There is a patch of grass
a little less green
where I pray
in the morning
and pour
some water
for my mom
my dad
my brother
my sister
my tired body
a prayer to the earth
for compassion
today
to relax
into what is difficult to love
inside myself
and to let
the diamond edge
of my breath
slice open
the tough,
knotted places
that hurt
for attention
trusting
this discomfort
will ease
at the exact
moment
I choose
to stop

Becoming

Jackson Maloney

pushing back
against it
and allow
it to be
what it is:
a friend
in need
of water.

Becoming

Jackson Maloney

What You Are Becoming

Deep inside the heart,
there are arms lain open,
waving like kelp
on the ocean floor,
where it is so dark
things start to emanate
a light of their own.

This is deeper
than your yes
and your no;
deeper than
right
and wrong;
beyond the
complexities
of your self-expression
and the shame
and the guilt
that make you small.

This is about opening up
to the arms of the holy mother
of mothers,
the original
bearer of life,
a vessel of pure acceptance.

This is knowing
that these arms
hold back waves

Becoming

Jackson Maloney

that wait to break
from the center
of that deepest,
darkest ocean
towards the shoreline
that can receive them.

Our work is the preparation:
to make ready the landscape
that longs for wetness,
for the water of life.

And I want to know
if you are brave enough
to cast off the heavy net
of knowing
and let that water
that was your first home
before you knew
your breath
be the very thing
reminding you
of the love that you are
becoming.

Becoming

Jackson Maloney

From the Fire

I watch you walk by
fifty yards away
and it is hard
to feel lonely
with you so close
but I know
now
you are much further
away
and I am deep
in the fresh cut
of this aloneness
wrung by
the gravelly hands
of grief
like a rag
damp from
my own water
dripping
two feet away
from where
we light
the fire.

Becoming

Jackson Maloney

Sitting Outside Before Dusk

One star bright above me.
Music is coming from the neighbor's
house across the yard.

I have never felt so exposed
beneath the night sky,
as if I were the one lain open.

Clouds darken into familiar shapes
and then move away; the single star
still shining, alone, brighter now
as the blue starts to fade.

This makes no sense!
Grief, such a deep well
in the earth of my body,
and I am left looking up!

There is a hole inside human beings,
naturally, but what do we know?

We cry a little and move on
to other things.

Nobody knows who filled us
full of water, or why women
cycle with the moon.

We simply see the ladder
disappearing into the dark
black depths beneath us
and choose to descend.

Becoming

Jackson Maloney

The Work

Step into the shadow cast
by your own body, with your back
to the sun,

and feel the extension of your pain
projected onto the world;
onto women and animals
and other men.

Look at it closely:
ghosts appear from the past
in the forms of all of the people
who hurt you,
and you can see the thorns
in your own skin
are now swollen and
infected.

Go deep into the raw, pulpy flesh
of your wounds; your life
waits next to tear-water.

Everything you have wished
to disown
is now arriving back
at your front door
asking for reclamation.

Do not turn away.

Becoming

Jackson Maloney

You know better. You know
the histories of man; you
have read books and heard the stories
of those who let their inner rage burn wild,
decimating the fertile, virgin grounds of
their children.

Weep for them, and for the child
in you, too, who had to run away.

Then, with a gentleness learned only
from knowing your own capacity
to inflict pain,

allow yourself to drop
a little further
into the soft, damp place
the earth has made for you.

You are coming home.

Becoming

Jackson Maloney

Our Fathers

Sitting at lunch
across
from my supervisor
trying to hide
the tear in my heart
I tell him
I am leaving for
Lucky's market
and drive
to the park
near the job site
kneeling
in the grass
trying to coax
that evasive gremlin
of grief
in my heart
out of hiding
saying
for one of
the first times
in my adult life
it is safe enough
to feel this
talking
not only to myself
but to all the men
behind me:
my dad
my grandpop
those I never

Becoming

Jackson Maloney

got to meet
those
who were never guided
into the dark,
unchartered waters
of the heart
and I thank
each and every
one of them
for the sacrifices
they made
so that I could live
to see this day
where what was dying
in me
came alive again
in the mystery
of feeling broken
because as men
we were taught
not to show
our susceptibility
to pain
to getting hurt
by those
we love
those
we lose
so we keep
what was never meant
to stay hidden

Becoming

Jackson Maloney

inside
to rot away
but I will not
carry that story
any longer
because I love my dad
that much
I love my brother
that much
I love myself
that much
I will love my son
that much.

Becoming

Old Knowledge

Above the ancient bell tower
and the buzz of today's traffic,
there is a resounding silence
from where you were born.

This is not a religious statement;
this is a truth you know
deep down in your soul.

This is you
rocking back and forth
on the crest of waves
surrounded by nothing
but water
in the small boat
of your body.

This is god
and forever after.

Becoming

Jackson Maloney

Dragonfly

Down beneath
the water
on the bottom
of the glass
I saw a dragonfly
dancing
in the center
made of dust,
moving beneath
the clear liquid,
and I felt you there
with me
the way you were
all along
your presence
your medicine
saving my life
helping me
become
a humble man.

Becoming

Jackson Maloney

Surrender

Inside me, there are waves
brushing up against the silence.

They soothe me in my aloneness.

Stirring in me are memories,
old and intimate
glimmering like glass along
the sea-bottom.

Sun and wind have worn me thin,
though I never held much against
the open sky, anyway.

But now, I am soft enough to bend
leaning into you like a child,
no strength left to brace myself
against you,

my quiet body an opening,
an offering
for life to dance again.

Becoming

Jackson Maloney

Moving Towards Life

I come to the water today
because I want to give something back.

I want to give back the clumped up tears
hardened in my throat; the sadness, the
longing for death, the numbness of
not knowing the earth.

I come to see the strong bodies of the
cottonwood trees, moving fully towards
the sun, their tough, ridged bark
bearing the intensity of winter storms,
their green summer leaves
shimmering in the light of late May,
dancing freely in the warm wind.

I come to remember that their life
is my life, too, and the water
from which they drink
is the same source nourishing me
after losing you.

Today, I am choosing
to let my grief go…

…back to the stones and the
grass, to the trees and the running water
and the wind, to the wisdom of old,
earthen things that can handle much
more sorrow than me.

I cannot hold what the mountains can hold;
I cannot hold this in.

Becoming

Becoming

Jackson Maloney

My First Garden

When the first sprouts poked through
the dirt, I was astounded. But how!
Just from a puny little seed.

I looked at the sun.
I thought of my mother.

I was once a little seed, too.
Now, grown with hands that
grip tools, cook food, fold
the laundry.

But how much care it took to get me here!
Praise my parents!

Becoming

Jackson Maloney

Welcoming You In

When I see the white moon at night shining
or sit after a long day's work
in the quiet comfort of my garden,
something feathery moves
in my chest,
like a breeze I cannot grasp,
and I welcome you back in.

At first, I was angry,
feeling so much
in losing you,

not knowing
how to stand in the fire
of my loneliness,

or how to hold
the intensity of storms
inside me.

But as I am breaking open,
my tears are healing me
in the most mysterious way,
and that soft, vulnerable place –
the place in my heart
that you opened up with
your fierce love –
is the source from where I now draw
my strength
to meet the world again
in a fresh, exciting way.

And I am so alive
in knowing you!

Becoming

Jackson Maloney

Beneath the Fire

Have you ever allowed someone
to reach far down inside your heart
past the flame of passion and Eros
into the dark, swaying water
that shaped you?

That is a sacred thing!

Not any hand has that power
to reach so far inside.

Honor those that can touch you
so deeply as that!

They are the ones holding the sand
from the inner shoreline
where you first leapt into life.

They are the doorways
into remembering your true home
the core of the core
of the earth,
ancient star-being
that you are!

Becoming

Jackson Maloney

What We Deserve

There is an odd way
that we can say
thank you
to that part of ourselves
that did it what it could
to find the nourishment
of love
it needed as a child
even when that meant
giving up
essential pieces
of who we are
because it knew that this world
was too harsh
and too uninviting
without the comfort
of human love
and acceptance

but at a certain point
this changed because
we realized
that another part of us
needed water
too
and we remembered
what we had done
when we were younger
what we had given up
to fit in
so we learned

Becoming

Jackson Maloney

how to say
sorry
to that outcast part
of our soul
and began to welcome back in
those pieces
of us
that never knew love

and now
after all the grief
and all the tears
we wept
we find ourselves
saying thank you
and we begin
to deepen
our faith
for the first time
into our own heart
and find a love there
more vast
than we ever could have imagined
for ourselves
and we realize
we have deserved to feel
this big
all along.

Becoming

Jackson Maloney

Sea Glass

Pt. 1
We take glass shards
from the sea
of our hearts

and throw them into the ocean
of this world.

The waves carry them for a long
time, turning them over and over again,
through wind and salt and sun,

until one day they wash up
on a beach across the earth
worn soft from the sand,
translucent, green, and smooth.

Pt. 2
Soon, a young man
will be walking
along the sand
where the water breaks
on that beach across
the earth,
looking out
over the waves
for a sign of life,

and at his feet
he will find a single shard,
polished down by the mad sea,

Becoming

Jackson Maloney

and feel the weight
of its journey taken.

Pt. 3
In the smoothness
of that glass, he will remember
somewhere deep in the recesses
of his own body,

that all the edges of his world
which seem to cut
so sharp
can be smoothed down
by the same salt
of his own tears
and he will kneel
with his head
bowed gently
towards the sand
and give back
the water
he no longer needs
to carry.

Becoming

Jackson Maloney

What Is Carried

Walking down
from the lookout point
above Calwood Retreat Center
where men gather
to find the dream
of their lives unbroken,

I see a vision of myself
as an older man,
standing alone
in tall, blonde grasses,

and I cannot help
but wonder
if images like these
have always been here,
just beneath the surface,

or if they make themselves
slowly, like footsteps
paved in the dirt,

changing with
each wind,
each rain,
eventually
setting themselves
in stone

for our children
to happen upon

Becoming

Jackson Maloney

years later
when they walk
into the clear
blue day
of our prayers
made real.

Becoming

Jackson Maloney

Passing a Crowd of People by Car

People cramming the bridge,
the bridge a sea of purple moving
towards the stadium,
the people chatting, laughing, looking
at their phones.

We cannot bear winter
like the trees –
standing openly
in the freezing rain.

One strong wind and we collapse!
I know none of these people.
A man holds a sign
asking for fifty cents.
I want to tell him
that I am glad to see him,
that I am sorry
it has been so long.

Becoming

Arête

We meet
today
face to face
on a high
mountain trail
to acknowledge
each other
as a friend
who has given something good
and true
in preparation for
us both
to stand alone
together
on the shaky edge
of this transition
and peer into
what awaits below
the tree line
in the wake
of what has been
and what
will come to be
the presence
of something
alive and
mysterious
dancing in the laughter
and the tears
between us
as a low rumble

Becoming

Jackson Maloney

moves closer
and dirt bikes
roar by
waking us out
of that dream
to walk
the slow road
back to your truck
breathing
more deeply now
into what
is waiting.

Becoming

Jackson Maloney

My Body Is My Prayer

I dance like people have danced
since the beginning of time.

I dance because my ancestors
are watching.

I dance because I am a human being
who wants to express something palpable,
raw, and alive – the sweat on my skin
and the lightning of my breath.

I dance so my feet may remember how
to walk softly on the ground
beneath me,

so my chest may open up
to receive the strength
of the sun.

I dance, and my body is my prayer,
my sacred offering to life.

I dance because this is my inheritance,
and this is how I can show my creator
that I am grateful
to be here.

I dance for the people
who cannot dance for themselves,
that they may feel this movement
in their bodies just as strong.

I dance
so I can know myself, dancing!

Becoming

Jackson Maloney

Crows

It was not until
I felt the heavy
waters of grief
black and strong
upon me
that I could wear
clothes of the same
color
and know its true,
terrifying power
protecting
and shattering me
at the same time.

Unpredictable,
the way waves
can save a small
boat
stranded out
at sea
by slowly nudging it
towards the safety
of shore;
the way
those same waves
can crack the wood
of that same boat
into splinters,
unrecognizable
thereafter
no longer the thing

Becoming

Jackson Maloney

it once was
before the water
ripped it
apart.

The color black
says to the world:

I am familiar
with the night.

I have stepped
through the low, trembling
lips of grief
and been swallowed
alive.

And I walked out again
different than when
I entered, shoulders
slightly bowed,
standing face to face
with the light of morning
wearing on my skin
what was rescued
from that dark, shiny
depth
the way crows' black
coats
glisten in the sunlight
the way they shout:
sharp, clear, and utterly

Becoming

Jackson Maloney

certain of themselves
so piercing it makes
you want to turn away
yet you cannot help
but hear
the simultaneous
invitation
beckoning you to join
the conversation
of life around you
and to feel
the hidden weight
carried by so many
day after day
that it summons a courage
you never knew you had
to speak up
and say:
I can and I will
hold some of that weight
with you
because even though
I might not know you
or like what you have done
I know what it is like
to swim in black waters
and I cannot deny
what we share together
in that darkness
from where we come
and how

Becoming

Jackson Maloney

we were thrust forward
into the harsh light
of our lives
still clinging on
to the night
which no longer
      needed us.

Becoming

About the Author

This is the first collection of poetry published by Jackson Maloney. He has a degree in English Literature from the University of Colorado, Boulder, where his first poetry class changed his life and his relationship with writing. He enjoys the early morning, his favorite time to drink something warm and write or read in that dream-like state between sleeping and waking. This book has been a long time coming – nearly two years ago since the first poems were gathered together in a slim, black folder. Besides writing, Jackson is involved in traditional and modern rites of passage work and men's retreats in Colorado, where he has lived since graduating from college in 2016.